INTRODUCTI

An Introduction to Veterinary Prac

is your practical guide to be used alone or as part of the BTEC Award in Veterinary Practice Client Care. It is designed to take you through everyday situations that occur in practice when it comes to communicating effectively with clients, and encourages you to apply this to your own work.

Although client care is part of your daily routine, the way that you communicate with owners can have a crucial effect on the practice; ranging from clients' level of satisfaction, to whether they decide to move to another practice, or even take legal proceedings. Effective communication can be the key to a successful business and your own job satisfaction.

Take your time to read through the scenarios and our advice, and then complete the exercises to help you think about how you and your team would tackle the problems that arise.

NAME:_____

An Introduction to Veterinary Practice Client Care

Mark Moran, In Practice Learning Ltd.

Edited by Jenna Maryniak
Cartoons by Keith Hensby
Sponsored by Pfizer Animal Health
© 2004 VN Times

VN Times
Veterinary Business Development
Olympus House
Werrington Centre
Peterborough
PE4 6NA
Tel: +44 (0)1733 325522
Fax: +44 (0)1733 325512
e-mail: vntimes@vetsonline.co.uk

Designed and produced by VN Times,
a division of Veterinary Business Development Ltd.

ISBN: 1 85054 199 X

Price £7.50

ABOUT THE AUTHOR

MARK MORAN has more than 15 years senior management experience with leading "Blue Chip" organisations, having had responsibility for more than 500 employees. He is now an independent consultant with wide experience of the veterinary profession.

He is a director of Vets in Business Ltd, where he provides business mentoring and support for partners and practice managers, as well as helping to deliver ViB's management training courses in subjects such as staff management, business planning, setting pricing and fees, and client care.

Mark is also project director for In Practice Learning Ltd, which has developed and delivers the BTEC award in Veterinary Practice Client Care. He is also author of the **VN Times** client care series.

Mark can be contacted through Vets in Business on 01458 210468 or via e-mail at mark@vetsinbusiness.co.uk.

CONTENTS

1: UNDERSTANDING YOUR LIMITS OF AUTHORITY

2: SEEKING HELP WHEN REQUIRED

3: ASKING THE RIGHT QUESTION

4: LISTENING EFFECTIVELY

5: OWNING PROBLEMS

6: TAKING RESPONSIBILITY

7: GAINING THE CLIENT'S CO-OPERATION

8: OFFERING ADVICE WITHOUT CAUSING OFFENCE

9: DEALING WITH EMOTIONAL CLIENTS

10: HELPING CLIENTS AFTER THE LOSS OF A PET

11: SEEING COMPLAINTS AS A SECOND CHANCE

PART 1: UNDERSTANDING YOUR LIMITS OF AUTHORITY

SCENARIO

LAST week Mrs Brown came into the practice to buy a large bag of the special diet she had been recommended for her dog, Mollie. Mrs Brown had used the practice for more than 20 years, and was well-known to all the

... I KNOW. IT'S A SHAME, BUT WE STILL CAN'T DELIVER.

staff. She had recently had her hip replaced, and although she could walk about and catch the bus, she was still unable to carry heavy weights.

Mrs Brown explained that she had run out of food, and her daughter, who usually collected the large bags from the surgery in her car, was away on holiday. Mrs Brown asked if she could have the food delivered to her home.

Peggy was on the reception desk when Mrs Brown came into the practice. She listened sympathetically to Mrs Brown's story and then told her that, unfortunately, it was not the practice's policy to deliver. She asked Mrs Brown if there was anyone else she knew with a car who might be able to help. Mrs Brown said she didn't like to ask other people. She then said that if the practice could not deliver she would have to buy the food at the local pet superstore which was quite near to her house, because a taxi from there would be much less expensive.

Then Peggy thought of a solution: she realised that she must live quite close to Mrs Brown, and so she offered to drop the food off on her way home.

Mrs Brown was of course delighted.

Q: What, in your opinion, did Peggy do well?
Q: What, specifically, did Peggy do wrong?

Peggy did a lot of things well. Firstly, she listened to Mrs Brown sympathetically. It is always important to show clients that you understand and sympathise with their problem. Then, when she realised that Mrs Brown's request was for something the practice did not normally offer, she apologised and explained the practice's policy on home deliveries.

7

Peggy then tried to suggest an alternative solution that would be acceptable to both Mrs Brown and the practice (did Mrs Brown know someone else with a car?). When this alternative was not acceptable, Peggy used her initiative in deciding that, in this case (to satisfy a loyal customer), some out-of-the-ordinary service could be offered.

She was then able to suggest an innovative solution, and she took responsibility for making sure that her solution was carried out (she would deliver the food herself). The result was that a long-standing customer had been satisfied.

On the face of it, Peggy seemed to do everything right. However, it was not the practice's policy to deliver, and in taking it upon herself to deliver, Peggy was not following the practice's procedure.

As well as ensuring that all members of staff act consistently, the other main purpose of procedures is to ensure that we act in our own and our practice's interest at all times.

Peggy did not have the authority to implement her solution, and she should have sought permission before agreeing to carry it out.

Because Peggy did not ask permission for her solution she was no longer acting as part of the practice team. Were she to have had an accident whilst making the delivery, she may not have been covered by the practice's insurance for either her car or herself. Also, had some emergency occurred that prevented Peggy from carrying out her promise, no one in the practice would have known to cover for her.

Using your own initiative is a good thing, so long as you keep within your limits of authority. Clients understand that all employees have limits of authority and will be happy to wait whilst you seek permission, so long as you explain to them what you are going to do.

Meeting the needs of the customer always has to be balanced with meeting the needs of the practice. In the above example, Peggy was right to try to find a solution, she was wrong to exceed her own limits of authority. Remember, you should never exceed your limits of authority, and if you are unsure as to just how far you can go, then always check with your supervisor or a senior member of staff.

EXERCISE

Your limits of authority may have been written down or may have been given to you verbally. How much authority you have will reflect your experience and position within the practice.

Use the space below to identify your main limits of authority. If you are unsure then talk about this with your supervisor, and record the result of your discussions below.

My main limits of authority are:

1. _____

2. _____

3. _____

4. _____

5. _____

PART 2: SEEKING HELP WHEN REQUIRED

SCENARIO

IT was getting towards the end of a quiet midweek evening surgery. The duty vet and nurse were together in the consulting room with the final client of the day, leaving Sheila alone in reception. The telephone rang, and Sheila answered it in her usually cheery way.

YOU MAY NOT HAVE ALL THE INFORMATION YOU NEED.

The caller was a client who Sheila knew well. The client explained that she had just returned home from work to find her cat, Suzie, had developed a bald spot about the size of a 10p coin.

The client explained that she had brought Suzie into the surgery the previous week for her vaccination booster, and that as far as she could remember, the bald spot appeared to be where the vaccine had been injected.

Sheila asked the client if Suzie was behaving normally or showing any signs that she was unwell. The client said that as far as she could tell, apart from the bald patch, Suzie seemed her normal self.

The client asked Sheila what she should do. Sheila knew it would be another 10 or 15 minutes before the vet finished the final consult, and she did not have sufficient knowledge to advise the client appropriately.

Q: How would you respond if you were Sheila?

Most client requests will be straightforward and you will be able to deal with them quickly, and without having to refer to anyone else. There will also be problems that are more complicated or demanding, where you will have to consult other colleagues before you are able to offer a solution to the client.

There are generally six situations when you will need to seek help. These are:
- When you do not have access to all the information that you need to resolve the request;
- The problem may be new to you, or very complicated, and you do not have the knowledge or expertise necessary to solve it. This is the case in this scenario;

10

An Introduction to Client Care

- You do not have the authority to implement the required solution;
- You have decided on a solution, but your solution requires input from someone else, and you need to check that person is going to be available;
- The solution you have proposed is unacceptable to the client, and you are unable to identify an acceptable alternative;
- The client is very angry or emotional, and you are unable to pacify or calm him or her down.

Once Sheila became aware that she could not provide a solution straight away, she would have to propose a solution that required the client to leave the problem unresolved. Clients want their problems solved, and so this is unlikely to satisfy them.

If Sheila is going to get the client's support for her proposal then the first thing she must do is to explain to the client why she is unable to resolve the problem immediately.

Firstly, get an agreement that an immediate solution is not possible. Sheila explains to the client that she does not have sufficient knowledge to advise the client in this case, that she will need to refer the matter to a vet and, at this time, there are no vets available.

Secondly, Sheila must explain to the client what has to happen to resolve the problem and how long she expects this to take. It is important that you are realistic in your estimate of the time the process will take. The client will want you to resolve the problem quickly, but you must not be drawn into proposing a time-scale that is unrealistic just so that the client feels better, or to stop the person pressurising you. It is better to be honest at the outset than to have to explain the delay later. Then, set out a realistic time-scale for what needs to be done.

Sheila explains to the client that the duty vet will be free in about 10 or 15 minutes time, that she has made careful notes of what the client has said, and she will talk to the vet the moment he becomes free. You will need to make it clear to the client that if the proposal is agreed, you will accept personal responsibility on behalf of your practice for ensuring the actions you have proposed are completed.

Sheila tells the client that she will call the client back within half an hour. This is called making a personal contract with the client. It is the difference between Sheila telling the client that she will call the client back, and telling the client "someone" will call her back.

Clients are much more likely to accept your proposal if they feel that you are going to ensure the problem is not forgotten or ignored once they put down the phone or leave the practice. If getting the help you require is taking longer than you anticipated, make sure you go back to the client and explain what is happening.

Using the knowledge and experience of the whole practice team is an important part of providing good client care. You are not expected to know everything, in fact no one does! Some client problems, by their nature, cannot be resolved without the help from another member of staff, and when this happens you should always follow the steps shown above.

11

EXERCISE

Make a note below of some of the people in your practice that you can go to and ask for help. Next to their names, make a note of any special skills or knowledge that you recognise they have. For example:

"Christine, practice manager – very good at handling angry clients."

Some of the people who can help me in my practice and the special skills they have are:

1.

2.

3.

4.

5.

PART 3: ASKING THE RIGHT QUESTION

SCENARIO

NIKKI was on reception one evening dealing with Mr Barton, whose cat Arthur had been in that day for a dental. One of the practice nurses had already returned Arthur to Mr Barton, and had explained that the dental had taken quite a long time because of the poor state of Arthur's teeth.

HOW, WHAT, WHY, WHO, WHERE, WHEN? ANSWER ME THAT ONE, MR BARTON.

She had also explained that the cause of the problem was almost certainly an inappropriate diet and this had convinced Mr Barton that he should purchase some dental products, and a trial pack of a "life-stage" diet.

Nikki entered the counter sales onto the computer, printed off the invoice and handed it across to Mr Barton. Mr Barton looked at the invoice, and the conversation went like this:

Mr Barton: "Oh, this is far more than I expected it to be, I'm afraid I haven't brought this much money with me. Can I pay some now and the rest later?"

Nikki: "You do know it is the practice policy that bills are paid in full on the day of treatment?"

Mr Barton: "Well yes, but I haven't brought this much money with me."

Nikki: "Your wife would have been told what the bill would be when she brought Arthur in this morning. Surely she must have told you what to expect?"

Mr Barton: "Well, when you put it like that, yes, but this bill is far more than she said it would be."

Nikki: "Could you leave Arthur here and go to a cash-point for the extra money?"

Mr Barton: "Oh yes, of course, I will go straight away, but I will leave the extra items. Can you take them off my bill while I'm gone and I will settle the rest."

With that, Mr Barton put Arthur on the counter and left. As Nikki sat down to make the changes to the invoice, she thought to herself: "I don't know why he looked so upset, I was only doing my job!"

13

3. ASKING THE RIGHT QUESTION

Q: Nikki was right in that she was only following practice procedure, but in doing so potentially valuable on-going sales of diet and dental products had been lost. So what had Nikki done wrong?

Once Mr Barton realised he did not have enough money to pay the bill, he had a problem. Solving clients' problems is what good client care is all about, but we cannot solve a problem until we understand it.

In order to understand a problem we need to ask questions, and the type of question we ask will determine how quickly we understand the problem, or, as in this example, whether we come to understand it at all. Choosing the right type of question is a key client care skill and, in this example, Nikki chose to use the wrong type of questions.

When we question a client, we are trying to establish what the problem really is and what the client really wants us to do about it, but in a way that does not cause the client to feel offended, yet makes effective use of our time.

There are three types of questions that can be asked, and it is important that you understand the difference between them and know which type of question should be used to gain the maximum amount of information.

The three types of questions we can use are usually referred to as **closed** questions, **leading** questions, and **open** questions.

▦ A closed question is one that generally invites the answer "Yes" or "No". In this example, Nikki's first question to Mr Barton ("You do know it is the practice policy that bills be paid in full on the day of treatment?") is a closed question.

Asking closed questions will not encourage clients to give you a great deal of information, and they are generally not helpful when you are trying to understand a problem.

Closed questions are useful when we want to confirm facts or to confirm consent. For example: "You first noticed the growth two weeks ago?" "Can you bring the flea collar back to the surgery tomorrow?" "Are you happy for me to speak to the vet on your behalf and call you back later?"

▦ A leading question is one that implies only one correct or desired answer. Nikki's second question to Mr Barton ("Your wife would have been told what the bill would be when she brought Arthur in this morning. Surely she must have told you what to expect?") is a leading question.

Some other examples of leading questions are: "I suppose you read the instructions, didn't you?" and "You did realise that it is to be given between meals?"

Leading questions should be avoided because they suggest that there is only one "correct" answer. This may annoy the client or cause him or her to feel offended. Leading questions may also cause the client to give a false answer, rather than risk being embarrassed in public.

14

3. ASKING THE RIGHT QUESTION

Leading questions can be easily avoided by asking the question in a different way and turning them into open questions.

■ An open question is one that requires the person being asked to really give the matter some thought, because it cannot be answered with a simple yes or no, nor is the answer implied in the question. Open questions will provide you with the maximum amount of information from a single question.

Open questions generally begin with "How", "What", "Why", "Who", "When" or "Where". For example, "When did you first notice the problem?" or "How have you tried to use it?" and "Why do you think that happened?"

Nikki should have asked open questions to explore the problem with Mr Barton. Did he think the bill was too much or was he genuinely embarrassed at not having the money with him; or, as Nikki suspected, was he just trying to avoid paying some of the bill?

By asking closed and leading questions, Nikki would have left Mr Barton in no doubt that she assumed that the problem was that Mr Barton was trying to avoid paying all of the bill, without trying to understand his situation. If this were not the case, Mr Barton would be right to feel offended.

The situation may also have been caused by the practice not clearly communicating the likely cost, or the additional costs that might arise if the procedure was not as straightforward as it appeared. In these circumstances, the practice may choose to relax its usual payment protocols.

Nikki should have asked open questions to explore the situation, such as: "What did your wife say the vet's estimate was?", "What other form of payment do you have with you?", "How would you propose to resolve this problem?"

If Nikki had used open questions she would have been able to resolve Mr Barton's problem to both his and the practice's satisfaction, without upsetting Mr Barton and losing valuable sales.

3. ASKING THE RIGHT QUESTION

EXERCISE

Write down three examples of "closed" questions that you could use in your work.

1.

2.

3.

Write down three examples of open questions that you could use in your work.

1.

2.

3.

16

An Introduction to Client Care

PART 4: LISTENING EFFECTIVELY

SCENARIO

LUCY had finished assisting with the morning surgery and was on reception duty covering the lunch-time period, when the telephone rang. Lucy gave the caller her usual cheery "Hello".

Lucy had been a VN at the practice for nearly 10 years and knew all of the practice regulars. The caller was Mrs Jones. Mrs Jones had been coming to the

I FIND MYSELF THINKING OF SOMETHING MORE INTERESTING.

practice for the past four years, since she had first taken on Molly as a puppy from the rescue centre.

Molly had suffered from quite a few problems with her digestion when she was young, and as a result had become well known to the practice team, as had her owner. Mrs Jones was "a bit of an old worry bag" according to Lucy, who had expressed this view to several members of the team following Mrs Jones' visit to the practice only last week.

The vet had recommended that Molly tried out a new "lifestyle diet" that the practice now sold. Mrs Jones had made Lucy go through the feeding instructions at least three times before she left the practice. Lucy could guess what was coming next. The rest of the conversation went like this:

Lucy: "How can I help you, Mrs Jones?"

Mrs Jones: "I don't know if this new diet is working correctly."

Lucy: "Oh I'm sure it's nothing to worry about. It often takes dogs a few days to get used to a new diet."

Mrs Jones: "Oh, but I am worried. Molly is usually such a good eater, and last night she left some of her food, and..."

Lucy: "Perhaps you have been giving her too much. Have you been following the   17 advice I gave you last week?"

Mrs Jones: "Oh yes, I've been very careful to make sure I give her the correct amount, but you see..."

Lucy: "Have you been giving her any treats or other food as well?"

Mrs Jones: "Well only the ones I buy from you, and I always make sure she only had two or three a day, but I..."

Lucy: "Well, as I said, it's nothing to worry about. Stop the treats if you think that might be the problem, and I'm sure she will soon settle down."

Mrs Jones hung up. "How rude," thought Lucy, she didn't say goodbye.

Later that afternoon Lucy took another call. This time it was from a neighbouring practice requesting Molly Jones's patient records.

Q: What had Lucy done wrong?

Before you can start to solve a problem for a client you must be absolutely clear about the nature of the problem. Some clients are able to explain exactly what is wrong, whilst other clients may give a confusing or rambling description. Some clients may be so angry or upset that it can be very difficult to get a clear picture of exactly what has occurred.

The most important skill you need to use when identifying the nature of a problem is being able to listen effectively.

In this scenario, Lucy was not listening! She had already decided what Mrs Jones was going to say and gave her answers without trying to listen to Mrs Jones.

Even though listening is a key communication skill, we often find listening with our full attention is something that is quite difficult to do. This is because throughout the day our ears are bombarded with thousands of messages in the form of both spoken words and other distinct and recognisable sounds. If we were to pay full attention to every sound that our ears detect, we would soon have brain-overload.

So, instead of paying full attention to every single sound, we filter out most of the incoming messages and only actively listen to those that we perceive as important at that point in time. This means that if, like Lucy, our reaction is one of, "Oh no, I've heard this before!" or "Here we go again!" then we can tend to become passive rather than active listeners.

Passive listening means that even though we may give the appearance of listening, we are actually paying very little attention either to the speaker, or what is being said. Instead we are thinking of other, "more important" things.

Lucy was fortunate that she was talking to Mrs Jones on the telephone, because our body language and actions usually show when we are not listening. The tell-tale signs of not listening include: avoiding eye contact, carrying on another task such as making records in the diary or on the computer, yawning, scratching, inspecting nails, hair flicking, or continually checking our watch.

18 Effective listening is a skill that you can develop. Becoming a more effective listener

will help you in all your dealings with clients. To see if you have a tendency to use passive listening on some occasions, try the exercise at the end of this section.

If you are honest, it will help you to recognise the symptoms of when you are becoming a passive listener, and you should make a special effort at these times to listen effectively.

Here are some tips on how you can become a more effective listener:

◆ **Concentrate.**
Effective listeners concentrate on the message and really try to understand what is being said.

◆ **Treat everyone the same.**
Effective listeners do not allow a person's status or personality to affect how well they listen.

◆ **Don't switch off.**
Even though the person speaking may be telling you something you already know, do not want to hear or something you disagree with, switching off or tuning them out will not help.

◆ **Don't make assumptions.**
Although it is often easy to assume we know what is coming next or that we have heard it all before, we can never be really sure, so don't make assumptions about what the speaker is going to say.

◆ **Don't try to think ahead.**
It is impossible to simultaneously concentrate on what is being said and think about what your reply will be. Effective listeners consider what they want to say after the speaker has finished speaking.

◆ **Don't mentally judge and/or criticise.**
It is impossible to give the speaker your full attention if you are mentally judging or criticising some aspect of what they are saying, their appearance, personality or mannerisms.

◆ **Don't finish the speaker's sentences.**
Even when the speaker is long-winded, confusing or confused, effective listeners never interrupt, talk over or finish other people's sentences for them. Yes, it can be difficult, but effective listening is hard work sometimes!

Finally, you should remember that we have two ears and one mouth, so that when trying to understand a client's problem we can do twice as much listening as speaking!

4. LISTENING EFFECTIVELY

EXERCISE

How effective a listener are you? Tick the box that most closely matches your own performance.

When I am listening to someone else I:

	Often	Sometimes	Never
– Find myself thinking of something else ...	☐	☐	☐
– Pay less attention to some people than I would to others ...	☐	☐	☐
– Pay no attention to some people if I am not interested ...	☐	☐	☐
– Try to guess what they will say next ...	☐	☐	☐
– Try to think about what I am going to say in reply ...	☐	☐	☐
– Try to look interested whilst thinking of something else more important ...	☐	☐	☐
– Try to judge the person by looking at their dress, mannerisms or body language ...	☐	☐	☐
– Interrupt the speaker to save time if I know what they are going to say next ...	☐	☐	☐

Effective listeners will have answered "never" to all of the above questions, although most people will have marked "sometimes" on at least two of them. You should try not to do any of the above and give your client your undivided attention.

20

An Introduction to Client Care

PART 5: OWNING PROBLEMS

SCENARIO

DURING her lunch hour, Pauline bought a medicated cat collar from her usual veterinary practice, which was in the centre of the town where she worked.

That evening she put the elasticated flea collar on her cat following the manufacturer's instructions, and she was careful to ensure that she washed her hands afterwards.

LOOK, SHE'S A CAT, AND THAT'S OBVIOUSLY A DOG COLLAR.

The following day when Pauline returned home from work, she noticed that her cat was not steady on its legs and seemed quite listless. Remembering what she had read in the instructions, Pauline immediately took the collar off the cat and kept an eye on her. The next morning, much to Pauline's relief, the cat seemed fine.

It was a couple of days before Pauline could get away at lunchtime, but she returned to the practice with the collar and spoke to Jenny the receptionist. She explained what had happened and then the conversation went like this:

Pauline: "So what are you going to do about it?"

Jenny: "Perhaps it was something the cat picked up and ate."

Pauline: "She is a house cat and I haven't changed her food."

Jenny: "It most probably will be something she ate."

Pauline: "I said I haven't changed her food! Look, I don't think you understand what I'm saying."

Jenny: "Well anyway, you'll need to talk to Sylvia the nurse, and she's on her lunch."

Pauline: "Yes, and so am I, but what are you going to do about it?"

Jenny: "As I said, you'll need to talk to Sylvia. Can you come back after lunch?"

Pauline: "No I can't!"

Jenny: "Well I'm sorry, I can't do anything. You'll have to speak to Sylvia and she won't be back from lunch until gone 2 o'clock, knowing her."

Pauline: "Look, let's just forget I came in, goodbye!"

21

5. OWNING PROBLEMS

Q: What, in your opinion, did Jenny do wrong?
Q: What, specifically, should Jenny have done differently?

In this example Jenny broke nearly all of the rules for good client care!

Firstly, Jenny did not try to understand Pauline's problem. By immediately implying that the cat's food might be the cause, Jenny was telling Pauline that she was wrong in thinking the collar was to blame.

Even though Jenny was correct in stating that it might be something other than the collar, because she did not try to understand the problem as the client saw it, she created a confrontational situation. Understanding the problem means showing the client that you understand their problem, as he or she sees it.

Secondly, Jenny did not acknowledge the problem and apologise on behalf of the practice. Remember that apologising does not mean accepting liability, it means letting the client know you are sorry that he or she has had cause to complain.

And finally, Jenny did not accept responsibility on behalf of the practice for resolving the complaint. Instead, she tried to pass the problem straight onto someone else.

When a client makes a complaint, you should always show the client that you:

✔ Understand the problem;

✔ Acknowledge the problem;

✔ Accept responsibility for the problem on behalf of your practice.

To show someone that you understand what he or she has said, you can summarise the key points of the conversation, or you can ask questions to confirm the facts. For example, in this case Jenny could have said: "So you noticed that your cat was a little listless after she had worn the collar for a day or so?"

Summarising gives the client the opportunity to correct any misunderstandings, to clarify what they have said, and to provide additional information that they may have forgotten. So, for the above example Pauline might have replied: "Yes, and she was not walking very well."

Acknowledging the problem does not mean accepting liability, and you must be careful not to give the client the impression that you are. Instead, it involves showing the client that you recognise that there is a problem, and it is understandable that he or she is upset, angry, inconvenienced, or whatever.

Accepting responsibility for the problem means you take personal ownership of the problem and for putting it right, rather than attempting to pass the buck to someone else. It is the difference between: "You'll have to come back when the person who served you is here," and, "I will need to bring this matter to the attention of the practice manager. I will see her this afternoon and I will call you to let you know the outcome."

5. OWNING PROBLEMS

The key point is that when a client has a problem, he or she wants you to take responsibility for finding a solution. Clients recognise that you may not have the authority to resolve their problem immediately and you may have to refer the matter to someone else. They will welcome your support in getting their problem solved and having their difficulties sorted out as quickly, easily and as smoothly as possible.

Obviously, you should never make promises you cannot keep, and you must follow your own practice's systems and procedures for dealing with client returns, complaints and so on. Nevertheless, it is always important to show clients that you understand, acknowledge and own the problem, and you will help to sort it out for them, as far as you are able.

5. OWNING PROBLEMS

EXERCISE

Imagine that you are on duty at the reception desk, and that you have to deal with Pauline and her problem. Think about the responses that you would you give to Pauline, and make a note of them below.

What would you say in order to show that:

1. You understand the problem?

2. You acknowledge the problem?

3. You will accept responsibility for the problem on behalf of your practice?

PART 6: TAKING RESPONSIBILITY

SCENARIO

LYNN was on reception duty during a quiet day at the practice. A smart professional-looking lady entered and strode confidently up to the reception counter. Lynn did not recognise her, but from her appearance guessed she was a "rep" making an unplanned call.

I CAN ASSURE YOU, MADAM, OUR SYSTEM IS NOT PROGRAMMED FOR MISTAKES

As Lynn went through her cheery, "Good morning, how can I help you?" she was already thinking, "You're going to be disappointed, the practice manager is away on a visit and the duty partner is in theatre".

Lynn had guessed wrong, the lady may have been a "rep", but she hadn't come selling. The lady introduced herself as Mrs Tyler and asked to speak to the most senior person available, as she wished to make a complaint. Lynn politely advised her that she was the most senior person available and asked how she could help.

Mrs Tyler explained that her parents were Mr and Mrs Joyce, who Lynn immediately recognised as long-standing clients of the practice. Her parent's cat, Lady, had been unwell for some time, and last week they had reached the painful decision that it was time to end Lady's suffering.

Because her parents were so very upset, Mrs Tyler had brought Lady into the surgery for them, and had asked that the invoice for the euthanasia and individual cremation be sent to her home to avoid them any further upset. She had called on her parents that morning and found that the invoice had been sent to them, despite her request.

Lynn immediately apologised for the practice's oversight, and asked Mrs Tyler to take a seat whilst she looked into the matter. Lynn could see from the Joyce's computer record that a note of Mrs Tyler's instructions had been made on the file.

Lynn could guess at what had happened. The invoices were produced "auto- 25 matically" at the end of the month and would have been addressed to the Joyce's as the registered owners. Whoever had produced it could not have looked at the note on the file.

Lynn explained what had happened to Mrs Tyler, apologised once again, and assured her that she had made a written note of the complaint and would bring it to the practice manager's attention on her return.

Q: How could this problem have been avoided?

Lynn showed good client care skills when dealing with Mrs Tyler. She remembered to apologise immediately on behalf of the practice, sought out all the facts before responding, and she did not seek to blame anyone within the practice for the problem.

It is all too easy to point the finger of blame at one member of staff. Lynn was right to remember it was the practice that had let Mrs Tyler down, not any one individual. Lynn was also careful to mention that she had made a written note of the complaint, and that she would ensure a more senior person was made aware of it: this would have helped her to reassure Mrs Tyler that she would act on her complaint.

Lynn had correctly spotted that the problem had arisen because the person who put Mrs Tyler's request onto her parents' notes had assumed that whoever produced the invoice would see it there and act accordingly. In Lynn's practice, the production of invoices was an "automatic" process performed by the practice's computer system, usually at the end of each month.

In common with many practices, the invoices will have been checked to see that they have printed correctly, but there is usually no requirement for the person issuing the invoice to view the patient record files for each invoice raised. Making a note in the patient's record file was not sufficient to ensure that the client's request was met.

In this example, the individual concerned was clearly unaware of the practice's procedure for issuing invoices. Yet we cannot reasonably expect every member of staff to know the detail of every process or procedure the practice undertakes, so whilst having an understanding of each other's roles in the practice is useful, it is not the complete answer.

The solution to this problem is to ensure that all members of staff are trained in how to react in these circumstances. We must ensure that all staff recognise that if they take a special request on behalf of a client, then they must take full responsibility for the actions of the practice until either the request has been completed in full, or another member of the practice team agrees to take the responsibility from them.

So, in this case, the person responsible had two possible courses of action. Firstly, he or she could have ensured that the instructions reached whoever was responsible for producing and mailing the invoices and confirmed that the responsibility had been taken by that person to ensure it happened. Alternatively, a better solution would have been to complete the task him or herself, if he or she had the authority to do so, and in that way ensured that the practice met the wishes of the client.

26

EXERCISE

Imagine that you were on duty at the reception desk and that you had to deal with Mrs Tyler and her problem.

What would you say in order to show that:

1. You understand the problem?

2. You acknowledge the problem?

3. You will accept responsibility for the problem on behalf of your practice?

27

PART 7: GAINING THE CLIENT'S CO-OPERATION

SCENARIO

AMANDA was "holding the fort" on reception when a client entered the practice with a rather lively Jack Russell pulling on its lead. Amanda was not expecting any clients as the afternoon session did not start for another hour.

Amanda greeted the client in her usual way and asked how she could help. The client introduced herself as Mrs Thompson, and told Amanda that she had an appointment with Sarah, the practice's pet behaviourist. Amanda immediately real-

... I WILL IF I CAN,
IF ONLY I COULD, THEN AGAIN
I MIGHT, BUT PERHAPS I CAN'T.

ised that there was a problem, because she knew that Sarah had gone off for the day with Judith, the practice manager, to visit a referral practice.

Amanda checked the diary that Sarah used for her behaviour appointments and could see that today's page was clearly marked "practice visit". Amanda looked up and said to Mrs Thompson, "I'm sorry, there seems to be a misunderstanding, Sarah is not in the practice today. Are you sure that you have the right day?"

Mrs Thompson looked deeply disappointed as she said, "My dear, of course I have the right day. I called only yesterday afternoon and the young lady I spoke to was quite clear that I could bring Roger in today. He's my daughter's dog that I'm looking after whilst she is away. I'm afraid he's causing a lot of damage around the house, and she kindly arranged this emergency appointment for me."

As Mrs Thompson was speaking, Amanda thought, "That will be Alice, the trainee receptionist, what's she done this time?" Alice had made quite a few mistakes recently. Amanda turned the page in the diary and could see Mrs Thompson's name marked in the following week. It was now quite clear to Amanda what Alice had done!

Before Amanda could compose her reply, Mrs Thompson added, "I really am at my wits' end. Just getting Roger here has been an ordeal. If it's all been a great waste of

28

7. GAINING THE CLIENT'S CO-OPERATION

time I shall be very upset. What on earth was that girl thinking about when she told me to come along today? Surely there's something you can do to help?"

Q: Mrs Thompson cannot see Sarah, so what techniques can Amanda use to get Mrs Thompson to agree with an alternative proposal?

Solving a client's problem usually involves getting the client to agree with your proposed solution, or with the method you are proposing to reach the solution.

When a client raises a complaint, your first reaction, like Amanda's, is often to think "Who is to blame?" or "How did this happen?" Whilst finding the answers to these questions is important to the practice so that the problem can be prevented from happening in the future, it does not help the client. So when a client raises a complaint, try to think how to solve the problem, rather than laying the blame.

This technique becomes important when, like Amanda, you realise somebody has made a mistake that has caused the problem. It would be very easy for Amanda to launch into a great apology and tell the client how prone Alice is to making errors or omissions. Whilst this might make Amanda feel better because it puts the blame clearly on Alice, it does not help the client.

So when a client complains, give a simple apology on behalf of the practice, such as, "I'm sorry Mrs Thompson, but we seem to have made a mistake and have put your appointment in the diary for next week," and get on with solving the problem. The internal inquest can take place later.

Handling a complaint is quite simple when you can solve the problem straight away. However, in this case, Amanda knows that Sarah is not in the practice, so she will need to get Mrs Thompson to agree to another solution. The easiest way to get the co-operation of a client is to agree to do what they want!

Some clients will complain and then demand a particular solution. In these cases, even if you cannot agree because the client's demands are unreasonable, you at least have the starting point for a negotiation. However, often a client will approach you with a complaint and will not make any suggestions for how he or she wants the problem to be resolved.

Before suggesting your own solution, ask the client what he or she would like to see happen, because when you are handling a complaint it is easy to overlook an obvious solution. In many cases, you will find that the client's proposed solution is either the same as the one you were about to propose, or it may even be simpler. Because you are now able to agree with the client's proposal, you are assured of his or her co-operation.

Amanda asked Mrs Thompson what she would like to do. Mrs Thompson said that she needed help, and would like to see someone as soon as possible. On the occasions when you can't do exactly what the client would like you to do, try to suggest more than one alternative solution.

Giving the client a choice of alternatives reinforces the message that you are trying 29

An Introduction to Client Care

to help and lets the client participate in choosing the solution. It will also give you the opportunity to explore how much flexibility the client is prepared to accept in finding a solution.

When proposing solutions or alternatives, always use "positive" language. The client will have more confidence in your proposals if you use language such as: "I will" or "I can", instead of "I could", "I might" or "I don't know if ...".

Using positive language sounds as if you are really doing something, and therefore reassures the client. Negative language leaves the client wondering if anything can or will be done.

Amanda could offer Mrs Thomson a choice of solutions using positive language by saying, "I can go and see if Lisa – one of our nurses who sometimes helps Sarah – is free to see you now, or I can arrange for you to see Sarah as soon as possible tomorrow morning."

Finally, if an agreement is reached with clients on how you are going to proceed, be sure to thank them for their co-operation. After all, what they have just agreed to is not what they wanted, or expected, to happen in the first place.

30

EXERCISE

Change the following statements to make them "positive".

1. "I'm sorry, but you will have to see the practice manager."

2. "I don't think that Mr Robinson is in the practice at the moment."

3. "We don't know where he is at the moment; perhaps you could call again later?"

4. "If you want to leave your name, then we may be able to find out some more information for you."

PART 8: OFFERING ADVICE WITHOUT CAUSING OFFENCE

SCENARIO

EMILY, a qualified veterinary nurse, was helping to cover reception during a busy Monday morning surgery. The waiting room was quite full because Stephen, the newly qualified vet, was running late. As a result, a small queue had formed around the reception desk.

Emily turned to greet the next client – a smartly

THIS STUFF YOU SOLD
ME HASN'T WORKED.

dressed lady in her thirties, who Emily did not recognise as a practice regular. "Good morning," said Emily, "I'm sorry you have had to wait. How can I help you?"

The client responded by saying, rather too loudly, "I bought this flea spray from you three weeks ago and it hasn't worked. My cat still has fleas and they are all over the house."

To Emily it felt like the whole waiting room had fallen silent at just that moment and that everyone in the room was now looking directly at her. She tried to gather her thoughts quickly, becoming increasingly conscious of the growing silence. "I'm sorry that you feel the product we supplied you hasn't worked," said Emily. Knowing that the reception desk in a full waiting room was not the best place to resolve this client's problem, she went on, "If you would just like to come with me, I will take all the details and see how we can resolve this to your satisfaction," and with that she led the client into the nurses' consultation room which was unoccupied.

"Now," said Emily with relief as she shut the door on the dozen or so pairs of eyes that had appeared to follow her every step, "if you could just explain to me what has happened, I'm sure we can sort the problem out."

The client explained that about three weeks ago she had noticed fleas around the house. She had called into the surgery and explained to the receptionist that she had

An Introduction to Client Care

fleas on her furniture and had purchased the household spray that the receptionist recommended.

She had used the product as prescribed on the can, but three weeks on, the fleas were still visible and active. Emily knew the product the client had bought was effective because she had used it herself. She suspected something else was at the root of this problem.

Emily asked the client what form of flea treatment she was using for her cat. The client replied that she had bought a spot-on flea treatment from the supermarket when she had first noticed the fleas, and had then come to the practice when that did not appear to solve the problem.

Emily now knew the cause of the problem, and after a few more questions were answered, it was clear that a simple household spray was not going to cure it. Emily took a few moments to explain to the client the life-cycle of the flea, and how the various products available were used to control different parts of the cycle.

Following a little more discussion, Emily led a smiling client back to the reception desk to pay for her new purchases.

Q: Think of a similar situation that has happened in your practice. How was it resolved?

Emily demonstrated good client care skills when dealing with this client. She apologised immediately, and she remained professional by not letting her personal discomfort show when the client raised her voice so that the other clients heard her complaint. She recognised that many clients are apprehensive about complaining, and as a result they quite often seek the support of others in this way.

By responding positively and showing that she was taking the complaint seriously, Emily provided reassurance to the client, who was then happy to leave the comfort of the group. When circumstances allow, it is always better to deal with complaints in a quiet and private space.

Inexperienced staff often find dealing with aggression difficult, even when it is as mild as in this case. As a result, they allow their personal discomfort to show, and this usually only serves to make the client even more apprehensive and more aggressive. Being able to deal with mild aggression of this type is a key client care skill, for which all your "front-of-house" staff should have received appropriate training.

In this case, it was clear to Emily that the client had not been advised appropriately on her first visit to the practice. The practice team member who had served her three weeks before had apparently recommended the household spray based on the client's description of her circumstances. Emily correctly suspected that her colleague had not tried to explore the full extent of the flea infestation and had taken the client's description at face value. Whilst many clients are very informed on matters such as flea control, it is important to remember that many are not.

Clients are often too embarrassed to admit a lack of knowledge, or will try to 33 restrict the conversation when discussing a subject they are uncomfortable with. As a result they present partial or incomplete facts, which can lead to inappropriate advice being offered.

However, we cannot assume that all clients are ignorant and launch into detailed explanations whenever an issue is raised. Many clients would find this approach patronising and demeaning.

To avoid this situation, Emily asked open questions to establish the full facts, and to clarify the client's situation. In this way, she was in a position to explore not only the extent of the client's problem, but also the extent of her knowledge. As a result, she was able to educate and inform the client without causing offence.

Providing clients with appropriate advice is not just as simple as knowing the facts yourself, although this is clearly important. You have to be able to question effectively in order to interpret the client's situation correctly, and so apply your knowledge in the most appropriate manner.

8. OFFERING ADVICE WITHOUT CAUSING OFFENCE

EXERCISE

Write down how you would ask clients for the following information, in a way that is not likely to cause offence:

1. How often they use a flea treatment.

2. Whether they read the instructions before using the product.

3. The condition of any other animals in the household.

4. How often and where they exercise their animal.

PART 9: DEALING WITH EMOTIONAL CLIENTS

SCENARIO

ABBEY, a recently qualified veterinary nurse, was covering reception as part of her general duties when a middle-aged lady came into the reception area together with a terrier, which was pulling on his lead and rushing around in an effort to sniff every door post and chair leg.

Abbey recognised the client because she had been on duty three days earlier when Mrs Sharman had brought in Fleck with a nasty open wound on his hind leg. Abbey came around the counter to greet Fleck, and immediately noticed that the dressing had gone and the wound was again visible.

... REMAIN CALM AND KEEP FOCUSED.

Abbey tugged on Fleck's ears and gently chided him. "Who's pulled his dressing off then?" said Abbey as she positioned Fleck to take a closer look. "Oh you little monkey," said Abbey when she could see the wound more clearly. "You've pulled the sutures out as well!"

"Yes he has," said Mrs Sharman, "and all because the bandage was far too tight!"

"Pardon," said Abbey "what did you say?"

"I said," repeated Mrs Sharman, "the bandage was on far too tight. He started tugging at it in the car on the way home. I could see it was too tight, and by the following morning he had got it off. Now the gash looks worse than it did when I first brought him in."

Abbey could see that the wound had now clearly become infected. Abbey could feel her anger rising. She was never the best at applying dressings in her group at college, but she was by no means the worst, and she was sure she had done a good job on Fleck. Yet, here was Mrs Sharman trying to blame her for Fleck's predicament.

"I'm sorry," snapped Abbey, "but I'm afraid that the dressing was not too tight. This has happened because you would not let us fit a 'Buster' collar."

"How dare you blame me for this young lady?" shouted Mrs Sharman. "This is

An Introduction to Client Care

a result of your incompetence!" Abbey was speechless.

"Can I be of assistance?" said a calm voice. It was Patricia, the practice manager. "You certainly can," said Mrs Sharman. "Perhaps it would be better if we went in here," said Patricia, as she led Mrs Sharman towards an empty consulting room.

Q: What could Abbey have done differently?

Abbey demonstrated good client care skills when initially greeting Mrs Sharman, but her lack of experience showed in the way she reacted to Mrs Sharman's accusation that she had caused the problem. What Abbey had done was to allow the dispute to become personal.

It would almost certainly have been a simpler situation for Abbey to deal with if it had been some other member of the practice team who had dressed Fleck's wound, because she would have found it much easier to remain detached. Whenever we deal with a client complaint we must always act professionally, even though this can be quite hard to do at times, especially if we feel unfairly accused.

It is possible in this case that Mrs Sharman had a genuine grievance, or that she was simply trying to avoid paying additional charges. However, it is also possible that Mrs Sharman's actions were the result of emotional anguish, and by blaming the practice she was trying to deflect attention away from her role in the problem, so as to displace her own guilt.

By taking Mrs Sharman's accusation personally, Abbey became emotionally involved and so was in no position to establish the truth, or to resolve the matter successfully. Abbey needed to remain calm and keep focused on solving the client's problem without allowing an argument to develop.

Being professional means that we remain objective, we question and listen attentively so that we understand the client's viewpoint, and we do not jump to hasty conclusions. This is especially important in cases such as this, where the client may be emotionally affected by the plight of their animal.

Emotional anguish might simply be the result of a strong emotional attachment, or it could be fuelled by a sense of guilt. Clients who are emotionally distressed will often act in a manner which is out of character. This type of behaviour can include constantly seeking reassurance for their actions, angry and emotional outbursts, and seeking to blame others.

Abbey should have immediately apologised for the fact that Mrs Sharman thought that there had been a problem, and then asked questions to establish the facts: such as, "When did you notice the dressing had been removed?" or "When did you first notice that he had pulled out the sutures?"

By asking questions Abbey could keep control of the conversation and provide reassurance to Mrs Sharman that the matter could be resolved to her satisfaction. Only once the emotion has been overcome, can the facts of the case be established and an appropriate solution found.

37

9. DEALING WITH EMOTIONAL CLIENTS

EXERCISE

How well do you deal with emotional clients? Try this quick test to find out.

1. A client who is upset raises their voice. Do you:

   a. Continue to speak normally.

   b. Shout back.

   c. Run away.

2. A client who has just lost their animal is crying in reception. Do you:

   a. Ignore them and carry on as if nothing unusual is happening.

   b. Take them tea and tissues so that the other clients can see that you care.

   c. Try to move them to a quieter, more private place.

3. A client is angry because the vet is running half an hour late. Do you:

   a. Tell them to sit down and make less noise because they are disturbing the animals.

   b. Apologise for the delay and see if another vet is available to see them.

   c. Deliberately try to ignore them and carry on dealing with your other client.

   Answers below.

Answers: 1 = a; 2 = c; 3 = b.

PART 10: HELPING CLIENTS AFTER THE LOSS OF A PET

SCENARIO

WENDY was on reception on a quiet Tuesday afternoon. Wendy had one eye on the clock because she knew that the vet, Paul, was due at the branch surgery and his final appointment was now running late.

The last clients were Mr and Mrs Green with their Labrador, Trudie. Unfortunately Trudie had been suffering for some time, and Wendy had arranged for them to have the last appointment because she knew that it was quite likely that Trudie would have to be put to sleep.

When the consulting room door opened and Paul the vet entered reception, Wendy was surprised to see him break into a smile. He explained quickly to Wendy that he had had to put Trudie to sleep, and rather than rush Mrs Green who was clearly quite upset, would she mind making the Green's a cup of tea and sorting out the arrangements whilst he went over to the branch.

Wendy said she would be happy to sort the Green's out, but could not resist asking

I STILL THINK TRUDIE WOULD HAVE LIKED A MORE MODEST MEMORIAL.

Paul why he was smiling. "Oh" said Paul, "you'll see. Mr Green has brought the plans he has drawn up for Trudie's grave and memorial in their garden. I think Mrs Green would appreciate your support in helping to convince him that a more practical solution would be better."

Wendy took Mr and Mrs Green through to the staff rest room. Although Mrs Green was clearly upset, she remained calm and composed. Having settled them down, Wendy took a deep breath and then asked Mr and Mrs Green if they had given any thought as to what they wished to happen to Trudie's remains.

Q: If you were Wendy, what advice would you give to Mr and Mrs Green?

At or near the time of the death of their animal, many clients will be in a state of shock and may be unprepared for the decisions they will need to make. By making 39 sure we know and understand the options that are available, we can help our clients at this difficult time.

For many clients one of the most difficult decisions they will have to face will be what to do with the remains of their pet after death. It is important that you are able to describe the options open to the client and to discuss with them the advantages and disadvantages of each method in a supportive, yet professional manner.

Burial at home used to be a very popular choice, but its use is now declining. For the owners of companion animals, the idea of burying their "friend" in the surroundings that they knew and in a place where the owners can visit each day remains popular.

Also, for many owners, taking an active part in the burial of their animal helps them to grieve. They find the process of selecting a "special" place within the garden, the physical task of digging a grave, saying their personal goodbye, and then selecting a suitable way to mark the grave all helps them to come to terms with their loss.

However, home burial also presents many practical and emotional difficulties that also need to be considered. The most obvious difficulty is that as the average garden size reduces, and more people live in properties without a garden, many owners will not have access to a garden suitable for this purpose – so Wendy needs to establish what sort of garden the Green's own.

Where a suitable garden exists, the owner may have problems actually digging the grave. It is recommended that the grave should be at least 1.25 metres deep (between three and four feet), and has to be large enough to contain the animal. This means that for a large dog like Trudie, in excess of one tonne of earth will have to be removed.

In country areas, the grave also needs some form of protection to prevent it being disturbed by wild animals. This is usually achieved by placing slabs of stone or concrete over the grave, either on or just under the surface.

Wendy needs to ensure that Mr Green understands what is going to be required and how he will arrange for this to happen.

Another consideration that Wendy should make the Green's aware of is what will happen to the grave if they were to move at some future date. It is unlikely that any future owner of their home would wish to preserve or protect the memorial of someone else's animal – although they may be fortunate in this respect.

Because of these difficulties, many owners who do not wish their animals to be cremated may prefer to use the services of a private pet burial contractor. Many contractors own and maintain private pet cemeteries, whilst others will make arrangements on the client's behalf with other contractors.

In addition to burials, many contractors can also make arrangements for memorial stones, trees or other memorial items to be placed on or near the grave. The services that are available differ widely around the country, and Wendy should have made herself aware of the services that operate in her area, and be able to explain these to Mr and Mrs Green.

40

Additionally, when owners elect to bury their animal themselves and euthanasia or death has occurred at the practice, the remains will need to be returned to the owner's home. In some cases, the owners will wish to take the remains with them, although most will not have come properly prepared to do so.

Many owners assume that they can wrap their animal in its favourite blanket and carry its corpse home. However, the leakage of fluids that occurs means that some additional protection is required. Usually the animal's remains will be placed in a special bag to prevent soiling, or placed on a plastic sheet and then wrapped in a blanket.

Your practice may be able to offer to store the remains safely and hygienically for a few days, whilst the owners make suitable arrangements for the subsequent burial. In some cases, the veterinary surgeon may wish to carry out a post-mortem before the remains can be returned. Wendy will need to make Mr and Mrs Green aware of her practice's policy on the return of remains.

To ensure that there are no misunderstandings, Wendy should make a written record of the disposal arrangements that she agrees with Mr and Mrs Green and give a copy of these to them before they leave the practice. Your practice may have a special form for this purpose, which also serves as a reminder to practice staff of the disposal options that can be offered to the client.

After the death of a patient, the details must be correctly recorded and the client records amended accordingly.

Almost all computerised practice management systems include an automated feature that updates the patient and client records automatically if a euthanasia procedure is entered. Usually entering these codes automatically switches off the reminders for boosters and worming and so on. You should, however, check with your supervisor before assuming that your system does this to avoid any un-necessary distress being caused to the client by sending out a reminder for their deceased animal.

Many practices now send clients sympathy cards, usually signed by the vet or the nurse, or both. Most use a tasteful card, whilst others prefer to write specific hand-written letters of condolence for long-standing clients.

Sympathy cards remind clients of the human side of the practice. They help to replace their last thoughts of the practice as the place where their beloved pet died and remind them of the on-going support that the practice staff have provided.

10. HELPING CLIENTS AFTER THE LOSS OF A PET

EXERCISE

Make a note below of the names and contact numbers of cremation and/or burial services available through your practice.

1. Private pet burials can be arranged in my area by:

Company name: _____

Contact details: _____

• Leaflet available in reception?   Yes ☐   No ☐

• Brief details of services available and likely cost:

  a) _____

  b) _____

  c) _____

2. My practice uses the following contractor for cremations:

Company name: _____

Contact details: _____

• Leaflet available in reception?   Yes ☐   No ☐

3. Make a note below of the arrangements within your practice for the storage and collection of remains.

• The storage arrangements in my practice are:

_____

• The collection arrangements of our contractors are:

_____

PART 11: SEEING COMPLAINTS AS A SECOND CHANCE

SCENARIO

LISA was covering reception and basking in the news that she had just passed her level 3 exams. Having already completed her portfolio, Lisa was slowly coming to terms with the fact that she was now a fully qualified veterinary nurse.

... IT MUST HAVE BEEN A DODGY BATCH.

Lisa was practising her new professional signature: "Lisa Burrows, VN" and trying to decide just how big to make the "VN", when a client entering reception with a noisy dog disturbed her thoughts.

Lisa greeted the client with an especially cheery: "Good morning. How can I help you?"

"I would like to complain about the last batch of flea treatment that I purchased from you a couple of weeks ago. I applied it in the usual way, yet my dog, Gem, is now covered in fleas and scratching and biting himself. I think it must have been a 'dodgy' batch."

"Highly unlikely," thought Lisa, "but I suppose I will have to go through the usual routine."

"We are sorry that you feel you have a reason to complain," said Lisa. "If I can just take a few details, I will try to resolve the matter for you."

Lisa looked up the client's records and saw that Mrs Osbourne had purchased the leading brand of "spot-on" treatment. From a talk she went to only a few weeks before, Lisa knew that the product was effective and reliable and it would be most unusual if Mrs Osbourne had been sold a "dodgy batch".

Lisa explained this to Mrs Osbourne and finished by saying, "So, as you can see, it is highly unlikely that you were sold a faulty product, it must have been the way you used it. I can only suggest that you purchase another pack and I will apply it for you now."

"I'm afraid that's just not good enough," replied Mrs Osbourne. "I would like to see a more senior person and have my complaint dealt with properly."

"As you wish," said Lisa, as she went off to find the practice manager.

43

11. SEEING COMPLAINTS AS A SECOND CHANCE

Q: What could Lisa have done differently?

Lisa demonstrated good client care skills when initially greeting Mrs Osbourne, and she did remember to apologise to the client for having to raise the complaint. However, Lisa allowed her initial negative thoughts about the client and the complaint to influence the way in which she dealt with the matter.

She made no effort to ask questions to find out exactly what Mrs Osbourne had done and she made no effort to provide reassurance that her complaint was being taken seriously.

How well we respond to a complaint is strongly influenced by our attitude to the complainer and how seriously we take the complaint.

When clients complain to you, and especially when a client complains about you, it is natural to have negative feelings such as "that's not fair", or "that's not our fault" or to feel frustrated by the client's expectations. Unfortunately, we often then let these negative feelings affect the way we deal with the client.

You must remember that when a client complains he or she is giving you a second chance to "get it right" and you must take the opportunity given to you. By thinking positively, you are more likely to reach a solution that will satisfy the client and retain him or her to your practice.

There is nothing more likely to make a client go elsewhere than having a complaint badly handled. Clients who have given the practice a chance to put things right will feel that they have had it "thrown back in their face" if the complaint is not handled well.

When a client recognises something as being wrong, he or she will start to suspect that other things may also be going wrong. Clients appreciate that even the best run practices will slip up from time to time and handling their complaint well quickly restores their confidence in the practice.

We must also keep in mind that complaints can also be helpful. Complaints give the practice an opportunity to learn how to improve, they help the practice see itself from the client's viewpoint and they give the client something positive to say about the practice.

When a complainer has received a satisfactory response, he or she will tell, on average, five other people and will talk about it positively.

Every time we have some form of contact with a client, whether face to face, by phone, or in writing, it is a chance to impress that client, build the relationship and encourage him or her to return. These points of contact are often referred to as "moments of truth", because at that moment you have the chance to either build or destroy the relationship that your practice has with a client.

A complaint is itself another moment of truth and one which must be used effectively. Research on complaints has revealed that clients whose complaints were dealt with efficiently and politely felt even more positive about the practice than they did when everything was right in the first place.

An Introduction to Client Care

EXERCISE

Write down three positive statements that you can say to yourself next time a client complains to you, or about you, to get yourself thinking positively.

Next time I handle a complaint, I will think to myself:

1.

2.

3.

Enjoyed this book?
Want to learn more about client care?

IF you have enjoyed improving your client care skills whilst working through this booklet, then you may be interested in developing your skills further, and achieving a nationally recognised award by completing the BTEC award in Veterinary Practice Client Care.

The course is presented in three workbooks, which, like this book, allow you to study at your own pace either at home or in the practice.

In the first unit you will learn the importance of basic client care and have the opportunity to develop an understanding of how you can modify your own behaviour to improve your relationships with clients.

The second unit teaches you how to avoid or manage conflicts between the needs of the client, the pet and the practice. You will also learn how to manage the end of the relationship when the pet dies or is put to sleep, and how to handle clients' needs sensitively following the death of their animal.

The final unit gives you the tools and techniques required to handle client complaints, such that the client's needs are met and the practice learns from the experience. You will learn how to maintain a professional manner, question and listen effectively, and understand the importance of accepting, acknowledging, recording and reviewing the complaint.

What successful students say about the course:

"I have found the whole course to be very rewarding."

"The workbooks are very relevant to everyday work (in the practice) ... which has enabled me to increase my skills and knowledge, whilst allowing me to put them to good use on a daily basis."

"I found the exercises and assessments well laid out and easy to follow."

"I have thoroughly enjoyed the course; it has made me think, and given me the confidence to handle what can be potentially difficult situations."

• For further information or to register contact In Practice Learning Ltd: telephone 01458 210818, or fax your name, practice, address, telephone number and e-mail address to 01458 210040.